© **DASHING DECEMBER**
BY SANDEEP RAVIDUTT SHARMA

Table of Contents

Foreword IV

Dashing December...1

© **DASHING DECEMBER**
BY SANDEEP RAVIDUTT SHARMA

Foreword

This book provides you with a list of 100 motivational quotes and thoughts about LIFE, churned out by my mind with the divine blessings of Lord Rama and Goddess Sita. **Life is all about going forward.** Shed the baggage of the past, feed positive thoughts to your wandering mind, become the innovator by putting in the best possible efforts and keep going with a smile. Through this book, I have shared with you motivational and encouraging words. Absorb the positivity and live a joyful life. I'm sure if you keep reading, referring, sharing these thoughts and quotes about LIFE, you may derive inspiration and develop a good understanding of various perspectives and facts.

"Feed positive thoughts to your mind, and you can do wonders for yourself and the world."

I sincerely hope, you will find this book amazing, interesting, rejuvenating, unique and a constant source of inspiration.

Thank You and Happy Reading.

© DASHING DECEMBER
BY SANDEEP RAVIDUTT SHARMA

© Copyright 2018 Sandeep Ravidutt Sharma - All rights reserved.
In no way is it legal to reproduce, duplicate, or transmit any part of this document in either electronic means or in printed format. Recording of this publication is strictly prohibited and any storage of this document is not allowed unless with written permission from the publisher. All rights reserved. The information provided herein is stated to be truthful and consistent, in that any liability, in terms of inattention or otherwise, by any usage or abuse of any policies, processes, or directions contained within is the solitary and utter responsibility of the recipient reader. Under no circumstances will any legal responsibility or blame be held against the author / publisher for any reparation, damages, or monetary loss due to the information herein, either directly or indirectly. The author own all copyrights.

Legal Notice:
This book is copyright protected. This is only for personal use. You cannot amend, distribute, sell, use, quote or paraphrase any part or the content within this book without the consent of the author or copyright owner. Legal action will be pursued if this is breached.

Disclaimer Notice:
Please note the information contained within this book is for motivational, educational and knowledge sharing purpose only. Every attempt has been made to provide the reader accurate, up to date and reliable complete information. No warranties of any kind are expressed or implied. Readers acknowledge that the author is not engaging in the rendering of legal, financial, medical or professional advice. By reading this document, the reader agrees that under no circumstances the author / publisher is responsible for any losses, direct or indirect, which are incurred as a result of the use of information contained within this document, including, but not limited to, —errors, omissions, or inaccuracies.

If you have further questions, contact on **Tel: +919969256731**
Email: sandeepraviduttsharma@gmail.com

© **DASHING DECEMBER**
BY SANDEEP RAVIDUTT SHARMA

Dedication

This book is dedicated to **Sita Ram**. Ram or Rama is one of the most important incarnation of **Lord Vishnu** while Sita or Siya is the incarnation of **Goddess Lakshmi**. Ram denotes our Soul, or the super consciousness, truth and virtue. Sita represents the ideal of feminine and spousal virtues and is known for her courage, dedication and purity. As per the ancient text of Ramayana considered sacred by people practicing Hindu religion, Lord Rama and Devi Sita are referred to as the perfect man and woman.

I hereby pray to Lord Rama and Goddess Sita, for the well being, love, happiness, strength, positive energy and success of my readers in their life. To please and evoke the powers of the Lord Rama and Mother Sita for the well being of the world, I hereby recite the following mantra...

"Sita Ram Sita Ram Sita Ram Jai Sita Ram"

DASHING DECEMBER

© **DASHING DECEMBER**
BY SANDEEP RAVIDUTT SHARMA

Tough situation kneels down before a calm mind.

© **DASHING DECEMBER**
BY SANDEEP RAVIDUTT SHARMA

Toss the coin only when you can't decide without any bias.

© **DASHING DECEMBER**
BY SANDEEP RAVIDUTT SHARMA

Hold the cliff of hope until you catch the rope of life again.

© **DASHING DECEMBER**
BY SANDEEP RAVIDUTT SHARMA

Nothing is something which we don't know but are curious to explore.

© **DASHING DECEMBER**
BY SANDEEP RAVIDUTT SHARMA

Taste the flavour of freedom by holding the cup of life with firmness and responsibility.

Embrace happiness but don't get attached to it.

© **DASHING DECEMBER**
BY SANDEEP RAVIDUTT SHARMA

Cowards plan revenge, braveheart forgives the other even after the win.

Be ready to change your perception about people based on your interaction and experience.

Your reflection is as good as you. Work on yourself and you can be better.

© **DASHING DECEMBER**
BY SANDEEP RAVIDUTT SHARMA

Follow rules in life without getting enslaved in the process.

© **DASHING DECEMBER**
BY SANDEEP RAVIDUTT SHARMA

It's easy to get angry but really takes guts to hold it and still smile at the other.

© **DASHING DECEMBER**
BY SANDEEP RAVIDUTT SHARMA

One sided argument can never give you a fair judgement.

© **DASHING DECEMBER**
BY SANDEEP RAVIDUTT SHARMA

Enjoy the feast of life with a joyous mind.

© **DASHING DECEMBER**
BY SANDEEP RAVIDUTT SHARMA

Most of us look at the winner for inspiration but forget or don't explore the real teachers who are behind the win.

© **DASHING DECEMBER**
BY SANDEEP RAVIDUTT SHARMA

Humility brings people closer.

Too much thinking stops you from doing things. Avoid overthinking.

© **DASHING DECEMBER**
BY SANDEEP RAVIDUTT SHARMA

Exploring opportunities need a positive mindset.

Don't look for faults but be kind to lift if someone falls.

Aspire to touch the Sky.

© **DASHING DECEMBER**
BY SANDEEP RAVIDUTT SHARMA

Freedom begins its journey through your mind.

© **DASHING DECEMBER**
BY SANDEEP RAVIDUTT SHARMA

Share your ideas with the right audience, and your enterprise gets rolling.

It's good to care for the other but without exerting any kind of dominance.

© **DASHING DECEMBER**
BY SANDEEP RAVIDUTT SHARMA

Take charge of your life, and you can cross over the tide.

© **DASHING DECEMBER**
BY SANDEEP RAVIDUTT SHARMA

Why choose to go through the back door when honesty is your hallmark.

© **DASHING DECEMBER**
BY SANDEEP RAVIDUTT SHARMA

When you are excited to find a job, it may happen that the right job finds you before you do.

© **DASHING DECEMBER**
BY SANDEEP RAVIDUTT SHARMA

Never make the mistake of comparing yourself with the other. Compare with own self and make efforts to improve.

© **DASHING DECEMBER**
BY SANDEEP RAVIDUTT SHARMA

It's better to talk with people who are interested rather than focus on the ignorant ones.

Kindness comes from the heart and not through your money.

Face your fear once for all and it can never trouble you again.

© **DASHING DECEMBER**
BY SANDEEP RAVIDUTT SHARMA

Let your knowledge see the world. Kindly share it with others.

© **DASHING DECEMBER**
BY SANDEEP RAVIDUTT SHARMA

Embrace positive thinking and make it your way of life.

Look at the big picture but don't forget to look for the artist's signature in the corner.

© **DASHING DECEMBER**
BY SANDEEP RAVIDUTT SHARMA

Think twice when you are about to take the risk but not when you are sure of the opportunity.

False ego never allows you to learn. Shed it in time.

Desires can fly without wings, but efforts need the knowledge to take off.

True love doesn't take hate notes.

Innocence reflects divinity.

Amazing performance creates a memorable experience.

© **DASHING DECEMBER**
BY SANDEEP RAVIDUTT SHARMA

Conquer your bitterness with words of forgiveness.

The festival of life is celebrated every day. Be part of the celebration.

Blessed ones are those who don't ask anything from the Lord but still get and live in abundance.

© **DASHING DECEMBER**
BY SANDEEP RAVIDUTT SHARMA

Claim your rightful place before it becomes home to the other.

© **DASHING DECEMBER**
BY SANDEEP RAVIDUTT SHARMA

Life derails you once a while, get up to roll again.

Your kind words can help you to connect with the world.

© **DASHING DECEMBER**
BY SANDEEP RAVIDUTT SHARMA

You need to act in time to make things happen.

© **DASHING DECEMBER**
BY SANDEEP RAVIDUTT SHARMA

Never kneel down before the crisis, face it head-on and you can win.

© **DASHING DECEMBER**
BY SANDEEP RAVIDUTT SHARMA

Life is all about going forward.

Facing hardship is never an option for many of us. To respond with a smile is definitely our own choice.

© **DASHING DECEMBER**
BY SANDEEP RAVIDUTT SHARMA

Going uphill demands real efforts. Those who are dedicated are rewarded with a brilliant view from the top.

© **DASHING DECEMBER**
BY SANDEEP RAVIDUTT SHARMA

Before you decide to build a watchtower why not try to find the culprit within.

© **DASHING DECEMBER**
BY SANDEEP RAVIDUTT SHARMA

Golden words are said once, but they echo throughout.

© **DASHING DECEMBER**
BY SANDEEP RAVIDUTT SHARMA

Wonderful creations of the Lord feel his presence forever.

© **DASHING DECEMBER**
BY SANDEEP RAVIDUTT SHARMA

Act deaf to system which just speaks but does nothing on the ground.

You can simply walk and need not run to achieve a peaceful march.

Rare are those who spend their life helping others to achieve their dreams. Be the one.

Music connects with the Soul. Listen to good music and enjoy soulfulness.

© **DASHING DECEMBER**
BY SANDEEP RAVIDUTT SHARMA

You can create a wonderful world. Believe in yourself.

The destination of one can be the start for the other.

© **DASHING DECEMBER**
BY SANDEEP RAVIDUTT SHARMA

Follow those beliefs which makes you strong and helps you to decide the righteous path.

Let the happiness flow and create ripples of joy for the ones who are paying attention.

© **DASHING DECEMBER**
BY SANDEEP RAVIDUTT SHARMA

Let your mind relax before it makes you decide to quit without trying.

© **DASHING DECEMBER**
BY SANDEEP RAVIDUTT SHARMA

Truth cannot claim exemption when it's time to reveal.

© **DASHING DECEMBER**
BY SANDEEP RAVIDUTT SHARMA

Build your reputation step by step but not by tarnishing the image of the other.

Self-transformation comes from the heart, and your mind accepts it sooner or later.

© **DASHING DECEMBER**
BY SANDEEP RAVIDUTT SHARMA

What started as a voyage may become your life mission. Keep going.

© **DASHING DECEMBER**
BY SANDEEP RAVIDUTT SHARMA

Cheer and tear are what the world does to today's achievers and losers. It's your brilliance which brings to you what you deserve.

© **DASHING DECEMBER**
BY SANDEEP RAVIDUTT SHARMA

Nothing reflects better than the light.

Those who dare to walk on the clouds are not worried about the fiery rains.

© **DASHING DECEMBER**
BY SANDEEP RAVIDUTT SHARMA

Life is a paper boat which you cannot row on your own but which navigates with the power of the Lord.

The seeker of truth is not worried about the false accusations.

© **DASHING DECEMBER**
BY SANDEEP RAVIDUTT SHARMA

Knowledge multiplies and becomes valuable when one has got the will to share it.

© **DASHING DECEMBER**
BY SANDEEP RAVIDUTT SHARMA

Don't blame the alphabet 'C' for creating CHAOS in your life. Remember COURAGE also comes from the same.

© **DASHING DECEMBER**
BY SANDEEP RAVIDUTT SHARMA

With simple thoughts, you can make something grand. That's just not the power of your thoughts but your finesse of execution.

Step on the stone of failure and climb to reach the summit of success.

© **DASHING DECEMBER**
BY SANDEEP RAVIDUTT SHARMA

Pay attention to your health in time, and you can keep your wealth intact.

© **DASHING DECEMBER**
BY SANDEEP RAVIDUTT SHARMA

Don't stop to write when the flow of thoughts has found its direction.

© **DASHING DECEMBER**
BY SANDEEP RAVIDUTT SHARMA

Nothing seems right when you lose trust. Do enough to maintain trust.

Value the ones who are with you rather than crave for the indifferent souls.

© **DASHING DECEMBER**
BY SANDEEP RAVIDUTT SHARMA

Follow your dreams and lead the world.

© **DASHING DECEMBER**
BY SANDEEP RAVIDUTT SHARMA

Don't wait for your Golden time to come, create it now through your innovative and sincere efforts.

© **DASHING DECEMBER**
BY SANDEEP RAVIDUTT SHARMA

Not everyone understands the pain of the other. Those who do should give their best to lift such souls.

Inefficient ones always seek someone to blame. Expose them in time and make them accountable.

© **DASHING DECEMBER**
BY SANDEEP RAVIDUTT SHARMA

The hope of living a better life swims through the dark tunnels of the lost World.

© **DASHING DECEMBER**
BY SANDEEP RAVIDUTT SHARMA

After you fall in love do not repent. Remember it was your choice.

Accumulate knowledge not just to promote self but to benefit the world.

© **DASHING DECEMBER**
BY SANDEEP RAVIDUTT SHARMA

Impatient ones do run even on an escalator.

© **DASHING DECEMBER**
BY SANDEEP RAVIDUTT SHARMA

Conquer your fears with a rope of courage.

Quit your desires if it is distracting you from the righteous path.

© **DASHING DECEMBER**
BY SANDEEP RAVIDUTT SHARMA

Be ready to receive the divine blessings from the Lord.

© **DASHING DECEMBER**
BY SANDEEP RAVIDUTT SHARMA

Be thankful to all those who contributed towards your success.

© **DASHING DECEMBER**
BY SANDEEP RAVIDUTT SHARMA

Set your goals and seek motivation to achieve them.

Every day is special for those who have learnt how to live it.

© **DASHING DECEMBER**
BY SANDEEP RAVIDUTT SHARMA

Humiliation and rejection test our resolve to win.

Look up in life and you will find happiness staring at you and waiting for your welcoming smile to be with you always.

Choosing to walk takes you to your destination and not the path alone.

© **DASHING DECEMBER**
BY SANDEEP RAVIDUTT SHARMA

Life showers Cloud of happiness

© **DASHING DECEMBER**
BY SANDEEP RAVIDUTT SHARMA

The goals of your life remain goals and not the achievement when you forgot the value of effort altogether. Put in the right efforts at the right time and you can win.

Spend your time with positive thoughts and you can win.

www.ingramcontent.com/pod-product-compliance
Lightning Source LLC
Chambersburg PA
CBHW070803220526
45466CB00002B/522